Table of Contents

Introduction 7

The ICO Mania: Explore the frenzy surrounding Initial Coin Offerings (ICOs) and their widespread appeal to investors. 7

Bold Promises and Ambitious Visions: Discover the alluring visions presented by ICO projects and the promises that captivated the masses. 11

The Dark Side Emerges: Uncover the hidden risks and deceitful practices behind some of the most infamous ICO rugpulls. 15

Chapter 1: Captivating ICO Stories 19

Rising Stars: Explore the meteoric rise of ICO projects that garnered immense attention and funding. 19

Ambitious Visions: Delve into the ambitious goals set by ICO ventures, promising to revolutionize various industries. 23

Allure of Quick Returns: Understand how the lure of quick profits enticed investors to participate in ICOs. 27

Chapter 2: The Deceptive Web 31

Red Flags Ignored: Examine the warning signs and red flags that were overlooked by investors in their pursuit of lucrative opportunities. 31

The Art of Deception: Unravel the tactics used by fraudulent ICO projects to create an illusion of legitimacy..35

The Impact on Investor Trust: Discuss the fallout from deceitful ICOs and how it affected trust within the crypto community. 39

Chapter 3: The Spectacular Crashes......................43

From Boom to Bust: Trace the journey of ICO projects that experienced spectacular crashes and sudden collapses. 43

Vanished Dreams: Understand the consequences of these failed ICO ventures on investors' financial well-being and emotional resilience. 47

Repercussions on the Crypto Space: Analyze how the high-profile collapses affected the overall perception of the crypto industry. 51

Chapter 4: Grasping the Aftermath.......................55

Facing the Reality: Witness how investors coped with the aftermath of rugpulls and financial losses. 55

Legal Battles: Explore the legal battles and efforts to hold fraudulent ICO operators accountable. 59

The Role of Social Media: Discuss how social media platforms played a role in both promoting and exposing ICO scams. 63

Copyright © 2023 by Ethan J. Monroe (Author)

All rights reserved. No part of this book may be reproduced or utilized in any form or by any means, electronic or mechanical, including photocopying, recording or by any information storage and retrieval system, without permission in writing from the publisher, except for brief quotations in critical articles or reviews.

The content of this book is based on various sources and is intended for educational and entertainment purposes only. While the author has made every effort to ensure the accuracy, completeness, and reliability of the information provided, the information may be subject to errors, omissions, or inaccuracies. Therefore, the author makes no warranties, express or implied, regarding the content of this book.

Readers are advised to seek the guidance of a licensed professional before attempting any techniques or actions outlined in this book. The author is not responsible for any losses, damages, or injuries that may arise from the use of information contained within. The information provided in this book is not intended to be a substitute for professional advice, and readers should not rely solely on the information presented.

By reading this book, readers acknowledge that the author is not providing legal, financial, medical, or professional advice. Any reliance on the information contained in this book is solely at the reader's own risk.

Thank you for selecting this book as a valuable source of knowledge and inspiration. Our aim is to provide you with insights and information that will enrich your understanding and enhance your personal growth. We appreciate your decision to embark on this journey of discovery with us, and we hope that this book will exceed your expectations and leave a lasting impact on your life.

Title: The ICO Boom and Bubble: Unraveling the Tangled Web

Subtitle: The Deceptive Web: Warning Signs and Illusions of Legitimacy

Series: Rugpulls Unveiled: Untangling the Web of Deceit in Early Crypto

Author: Ethan J. Monroe

Chapter 5: Rebuilding Trust and Credibility 67

Strengthening Due Diligence: Understand how the crypto community enhanced due diligence processes to avoid future scams. 67

Self-Regulation Initiatives: Explore the measures taken by the industry to self-regulate and protect investors. 71

The Road to Recovery: Learn about projects that survived rugpull accusations and rebuilt their reputation. 75

Chapter 6: Regulatory Waves 79

Regulatory Responses: Examine how governments and financial regulators responded to the ICO boom and the rising concerns about investor protection. 79

International Perspectives: Compare the regulatory approaches in different countries and their impact on the global crypto landscape. 83

Striking a Balance: Discuss the challenges of implementing regulations without stifling innovation and growth. 87

Chapter 7: Evolving Landscape 91

Shifting Paradigms: Reflect on how the ICO boom and its aftermath influenced the evolution of the crypto space.. 91

Lessons Learned: Summarize the crucial lessons and insights gained from the era of ICO rugpulls. 95

Embracing the Future: Look forward to a more mature and resilient crypto industry that incorporates the learnings from its past. 99

Conclusion 103

The ICO Boom Legacy: Analyze the lasting impact of the ICO boom on the crypto ecosystem. 103

A New Chapter: Emphasize the importance of learning from mistakes and building a more trustworthy and sustainable crypto landscape. 107

The Journey Ahead: Look optimistically towards the future of cryptocurrencies, taking with it the lessons learned from the ICO boom and bubble. 111

Wordbook 115

Supplementary Materials 119

Introduction

The ICO Mania: Explore the frenzy surrounding Initial Coin Offerings (ICOs) and their widespread appeal to investors.

In the early years of the cryptocurrency revolution, a new fundraising method emerged that captured the attention of investors and enthusiasts alike—Initial Coin Offerings, or ICOs. This phenomenon would later be known as the ICO Mania, a period marked by an unprecedented surge in investment interest and innovation within the blockchain space. The allure of ICOs was as compelling as it was controversial, promising a revolution in the way startups and projects accessed funding while democratizing investment opportunities for individuals worldwide.

The Birth of a Paradigm Shift

As the dust began to settle following the launch of Bitcoin, the first and most iconic cryptocurrency, visionaries within the blockchain ecosystem were quick to realize the potential of this transformative technology. Bitcoin's decentralized and transparent nature laid the foundation for a wide range of applications beyond digital currency, spurring the development of innovative projects seeking to disrupt traditional industries. However, these projects faced a critical challenge—finding the necessary capital to turn their visions into reality.

Enter the Initial Coin Offering. In its essence, an ICO enabled projects to raise funds by issuing their own digital tokens or coins, which investors could purchase in exchange for existing cryptocurrencies like Bitcoin or Ethereum. Unlike traditional venture capital funding, ICOs allowed startups to reach a global audience without the need for intermediaries, providing an unprecedented level of accessibility and democratization.

The Gold Rush Mentality

As news of early ICO successes spread across forums, social media, and news outlets, a sense of urgency and excitement swept through the cryptocurrency community. Investors were drawn to the prospects of being early backers of projects with the potential to reshape industries ranging from finance and supply chain management to healthcare and entertainment. The speed at which these offerings could raise capital was breathtaking; what might take months or even years of traditional fundraising could now be achieved in a matter of days.

But as the saying goes, "With great power comes great responsibility." The meteoric rise of ICOs, fueled by the potential for exponential returns, led to a gold rush mentality that wasn't without its pitfalls. The promise of quick wealth drew both legitimate entrepreneurs and opportunistic actors into the space, blurring the lines between genuine innovation and outright fraud.

Pioneering the Path Forward

As the ICO Mania reached its peak, a wave of optimism and enthusiasm reverberated throughout the global crypto community. Entrepreneurs, developers, and investors joined forces in a shared belief that ICOs could unlock new avenues of financial inclusion and reshape the economic landscape. Yet, with innovation came the challenge of navigating uncharted waters, without established regulatory frameworks or best practices to guide participants.

In the following chapters, we will journey through the highs and lows of this tumultuous period, uncovering captivating ICO stories, exploring the deceptive tactics employed by fraudulent projects, dissecting the spectacular crashes that left investors reeling, and tracing the ripple effects that reverberated throughout the broader crypto space. We will also delve into the efforts to rebuild trust and credibility, the regulatory responses that emerged in the wake of the ICO frenzy, and the lessons that continue to shape the trajectory of the cryptocurrency industry.

As we navigate the intricate web of the ICO Mania, it becomes clear that this era was both a testament to the transformative potential of blockchain technology and a cautionary tale about the perils of unchecked enthusiasm. Join us on this journey as we untangle the threads of ambition, deception, and innovation that defined the ICO boom, and discover the enduring legacy it left on the ever-evolving landscape of cryptocurrencies.

Bold Promises and Ambitious Visions: Discover the alluring visions presented by ICO projects and the promises that captivated the masses.

In the realm of innovation, the allure of the unknown often carries an undeniable charm. It's the dreamers, the visionaries, and the trailblazers who dare to tread uncharted waters that captivate our imagination. The era of Initial Coin Offerings (ICOs) was no exception; it was a time when startups and projects presented bold promises and ambitious visions that resonated deeply with investors and enthusiasts around the globe.

From Whitepapers to Visions

At the heart of every ICO lay a whitepaper—a document that outlined the project's vision, goals, technical details, and implementation plan. It was within these pages that projects conjured a future where industries would be revolutionized, and paradigms would shift. As each whitepaper was published, a story of innovation and transformation was woven, often promising solutions to challenges that had long plagued traditional systems.

Diverse Visions, Shared Hopes

The diversity of projects launching ICOs was as vast as the potential of blockchain technology itself. From decentralized financial platforms aiming to disintermediate traditional banks to supply chain solutions promising transparency and accountability, ICOs spanned nearly every sector imaginable. Entrepreneurs and teams passionately painted vivid pictures of what their projects could achieve, capturing the imagination of a broad audience eager to be part of something revolutionary.

Promises of Disruption and Empowerment

The allure of ICOs rested not only in the technologies they proposed but in the transformative power these technologies carried. Blockchain's ability to remove intermediaries, establish trust in a trustless world, and democratize access to financial systems resonated deeply with those who believed in the decentralization movement. The vision of a future unshackled by the constraints of traditional hierarchies and gatekeepers spurred a fervor of excitement that crossed borders and demographics.

Navigating Hype and Reality

As the ICO frenzy reached a fever pitch, the line between genuine innovation and overblown hype began to blur. Investors hungry for the next big thing found themselves navigating through an ever-expanding landscape of whitepapers, each more enticing than the last. But behind the excitement, questions arose: Could these visions truly be realized? Were the technologies feasible, scalable, and secure? Was the promise of a new dawn genuine or just another marketing ploy?

The Emotional Investment

Investing in ICOs wasn't merely a financial decision; it was an emotional investment in a vision of a better future. Believing in a project meant aligning with its values, goals, and potential impact on the world. The allure of participating in a movement that had the potential to reshape society fostered a sense of community and belonging, transcending traditional investment narratives.

A Journey Through Visions and Reality

In the chapters ahead, we will delve into the captivating narratives woven by ICO projects—their visionary goals, ambitious plans, and the genuine excitement they generated. We will also peel back the layers to examine how some projects fell short of their promises, leaving investors to grapple with the stark contrast between vision and reality. As we explore these stories, we will gain insights into the dynamics of hope and skepticism that underpinned the ICO Mania, shedding light on the factors that propelled some projects to success while causing others to falter.

Join us on this journey as we navigate the world of ICO visions, tracing the threads of innovation, ambition, and aspiration that wove together to create a tapestry of promise and potential.

The Dark Side Emerges: Uncover the hidden risks and deceitful practices behind some of the most infamous ICO rugpulls.

Amid the excitement and promise of the Initial Coin Offering (ICO) Mania, a sinister underbelly began to emerge. Behind the façade of innovation and transformation, a darker reality was taking shape—a realm where deceitful practices and hidden risks lay in wait. As the crypto community embraced the potential of ICOs, the allure of quick profits and the frenzied rush to invest provided fertile ground for unscrupulous actors to exploit unsuspecting participants.

Beneath the Surface of Promise

In the quest for revolutionary ideas and groundbreaking projects, it was all too easy to become enamored by the veneer of promise presented by ICOs. The notion of being part of a movement that could reshape industries and redefine economic norms fueled a fervor that often overshadowed caution. But as the saying goes, not everything that glitters is gold. As we peel back the layers, we reveal a world where some projects sought not to innovate but to manipulate, not to transform but to defraud.

The Art of Concealing Deception

Fraud, manipulation, and deception are not new concepts, but the world of ICOs offered a novel stage for these nefarious activities to unfold. Unscrupulous individuals leveraged the euphoria and lack of regulatory oversight to launch projects that were designed not to succeed, but to extract funds from unwitting investors. With flashy marketing, convoluted technical jargon, and carefully orchestrated social media campaigns, these fraudulent projects created an illusion of credibility, luring in even the most cautious participants.

The Anatomy of a Rugpull

At the heart of the dark side of ICOs lies the notion of a "rugpull"—an insidious maneuver where project founders abruptly abandon their efforts after raising substantial funds, leaving investors holding worthless tokens. The rugpull tactic exemplifies the stark contrast between the bold promises made in whitepapers and the realities that unfold when the façade unravels. As we dive into the stories of some of the most notorious rugpull incidents, we unravel the intricate web of deceit, tracing the steps taken to secure investments without any intention of delivering on commitments.

A Community Betrayed

The impact of ICO rugpulls extended far beyond financial losses. They eroded trust within the cryptocurrency community, sowing doubt and skepticism among once-enthusiastic participants. The sense of community and shared vision that had characterized the early days of the blockchain movement was undermined by the actions of those who exploited the trust placed in them. The fallout of these rugpulls went beyond monetary losses; it shattered dreams, shattered ideals, and raised questions about the ethics of innovation.

Lessons Learned Amidst Deception

As we navigate the dark undercurrents of ICO rugpulls, we must recognize that these cautionary tales hold valuable lessons for the cryptocurrency industry as a whole. The deceit and manipulation that marred this era highlight the urgent need for improved due diligence, transparent governance, and regulatory safeguards. Exploring these stories isn't simply an exercise in exposing deception; it's a critical step towards building a more resilient and accountable crypto ecosystem.

Embarking on the Journey

In the pages that follow, we will explore the shadowy world of ICO rugpulls, diving deep into the mechanics of deception and the impact on investors and the wider crypto community. Through these stories, we gain insights into the vulnerabilities of an unregulated landscape and the imperative to foster transparency, education, and responsible innovation moving forward. Join us as we uncover the untold stories behind some of the most infamous ICO rugpulls, shedding light on the darkness that temporarily overshadowed the promise of blockchain technology.

Chapter 1: Captivating ICO Stories

Rising Stars: Explore the meteoric rise of ICO projects that garnered immense attention and funding.

In the early days of the cryptocurrency revolution, a new frontier beckoned—one that promised to democratize investment, challenge traditional funding models, and pave the way for disruptive innovations. Initial Coin Offerings (ICOs) emerged as the vehicle of choice for a generation of entrepreneurs seeking to fund their visions and a community of investors eager to be part of the next big thing. This chapter delves into the captivating stories of ICOs that shot to prominence, capturing the imagination of both seasoned investors and newcomers alike.

The Birth of Buzz and Hype

As the blockchain landscape evolved, so too did the way projects approached funding. ICOs ignited a spark of enthusiasm that spread like wildfire across the crypto ecosystem. The allure of being an early participant in projects that promised to reshape industries and redefine the way we interacted with technology was irresistible. In this section, we explore the origins of some of the most celebrated ICOs—the projects that managed to bridge the gap between technical innovation and mainstream appeal.

From Zero to Hero: The Meteoric Rise

The rise of an ICO project from obscurity to prominence could be likened to a modern-day fairy tale. Developers and visionaries articulated their ideas with eloquence, presenting blueprints for platforms, applications, and protocols that were beyond anything seen before. The combination of compelling narratives, visionary leadership, and innovative technologies resulted in explosive growth, with contributions pouring in from investors across the globe. We explore case studies of ICOs that transformed from small-scale initiatives into globally recognized and celebrated projects.

The Viral Effect: Harnessing Community Power

One of the defining features of ICOs was their ability to harness the power of online communities. Social media platforms, discussion forums, and online communities provided fertile ground for projects to communicate directly with their potential backers. The vibrant discussions, fervent debates, and passionate endorsements fueled a sense of belonging and loyalty that extended far beyond financial investment. We analyze how some ICOs managed to transform their communities into fervent advocates and contributors, contributing to their meteoric rise.

The Lure of the Unconventional

ICOs marked a departure from traditional fundraising methods, and this very unconventionality often served as a catalyst for their success. The prospect of contributing to a project without the need for intermediaries or geographic limitations was an enticing proposition for investors seeking to be part of a borderless movement. As we delve into the stories of ICOs that defied conventional norms, we uncover the factors that allowed them to capture the imagination of a global audience.

The Fine Line Between Success and Overreach

While the meteoric rise of ICOs brought with it a sense of excitement and optimism, it also carried a degree of risk. Some projects successfully navigated the challenging path from idea to execution, while others succumbed to the pressures of unrealistic promises and overambitious goals. We explore how the fine line between success and overreach became a defining factor in the trajectory of ICO projects, shedding light on the factors that led to either triumph or downfall.

In the following sections, we will continue to unravel the captivating narratives of ICOs by delving into their ambitious visions and the allure of quick returns. By exploring the highs and the lows, the triumphs and the pitfalls, we gain a comprehensive understanding of the multifaceted world of ICOs—a world that was at once groundbreaking and precarious, transformative and tumultuous.

Ambitious Visions: Delve into the ambitious goals set by ICO ventures, promising to revolutionize various industries.

In the heart of the Initial Coin Offering (ICO) Mania, a spirit of innovation and disruption swept through the crypto landscape. Projects emerged with audacious goals, aiming not just to tinker with existing systems but to fundamentally overhaul industries that had remained unchanged for decades. This section delves into the inspiring stories of ICOs that dared to challenge the status quo, promising to revolutionize sectors from finance to supply chain management and beyond.

A Paradigm Shift in Progress

The very essence of the ICO model was rooted in the belief that blockchain technology could spearhead a paradigm shift, introducing greater transparency, efficiency, and inclusivity into traditional systems. In this section, we explore how ICO projects seized this opportunity to redefine industries and bring about transformative change. From disrupting established financial intermediaries to reimagining data management and supply chains, these projects aimed to reshape not just the way business was conducted, but the very fabric of societal interaction.

Blockchain for Social Good

Many ICO projects weren't content with merely generating profits; they were driven by a desire to create positive social impact. The blockchain's potential to enhance transparency, eliminate corruption, and empower marginalized populations became a rallying cry for projects aiming to leverage their technology for social good. We delve into the stories of ICOs that sought to improve sectors such as charity, education, healthcare, and beyond, examining how their ambitious visions captivated both investors and advocates.

Financial Reimagination: Disrupting Finance and Beyond

At the core of many ambitious ICO projects lay the aspiration to transform the financial landscape. Fueled by the decentralized and borderless nature of blockchain technology, these ventures aimed to provide individuals around the world with access to financial services that had previously been out of reach. We explore how ICOs sought to revolutionize remittances, lending, investment, and more, illustrating their audacious visions through innovative use cases and real-world applications.

Realizing Supply Chain Transparency

The supply chain industry, often plagued by inefficiencies and lack of transparency, was ripe for disruption. ICO projects stepped into this arena with promises to establish end-to-end traceability, reduce fraud, and empower consumers with information about the origin and journey of products. Through case studies of ICOs that tackled supply chain challenges head-on, we examine how their audacious visions resonated with stakeholders seeking a more accountable and sustainable global supply chain.

Challenges and Realities

While the ambitions of these ICO projects were inspiring, they weren't without challenges. Technical complexities, regulatory hurdles, and the sheer scope of their aspirations often presented roadblocks that required ingenuity and resilience to overcome. In this section, we explore the journey from vision to execution, shedding light on the trials and triumphs that ICO projects faced as they sought to turn their audacious dreams into tangible realities.

A Testament to Human Innovation

The stories of ICO projects with ambitious visions serve as a testament to human innovation and the determination to reshape the world through technology. These ventures didn't merely aim for incremental improvements; they reached for the stars, seeking to transform industries and challenge long-standing norms. Their boldness captured the imagination of investors and enthusiasts alike, propelling the ICO Mania to unprecedented heights and cementing the role of ICOs as a cornerstone of the blockchain revolution.

As we move forward in this chapter, we will explore the allure of quick returns and the factors that drew investors into the world of ICOs, ultimately leading to the frenzy that characterized the ICO Mania. By delving into the ambitious visions, we gain insight into the motivations and aspirations that fueled this revolutionary period and left an indelible mark on the cryptocurrency and blockchain landscape.

Allure of Quick Returns: Understand how the lure of quick profits enticed investors to participate in ICOs.

In the fast-paced world of cryptocurrency, where innovation and opportunity collided, the allure of quick returns became a driving force behind the Initial Coin Offering (ICO) frenzy. Investors, both seasoned and new, found themselves drawn to the promise of substantial profits within a remarkably short span of time. This section unravels the complex psychology behind the quest for quick gains and explores how the appeal of financial windfalls propelled the ICO Mania to unimaginable heights.

The Gold Rush Mentality

Human psychology is intertwined with the pursuit of wealth, and nowhere was this more evident than during the ICO Mania. The prospect of investing a modest sum and witnessing its exponential growth within weeks or even days resonated deeply with investors seeking to capitalize on a revolutionary wave. We examine the historical context that made the ICO Mania the perfect breeding ground for the gold rush mentality, exploring how this mentality both fueled and shaped the ICO landscape.

The Fear of Missing Out (FOMO)

One of the driving factors behind the allure of quick returns was the fear of missing out (FOMO). As reports of early ICO successes circulated across social media and news outlets, investors faced a conundrum: jump on the bandwagon or risk being left behind. The fear of not capitalizing on what appeared to be an unprecedented investment opportunity led to a surge in participation, further fueling the ICO frenzy. We delve into the psychological underpinnings of FOMO and its impact on investor behavior.

Tokenomics and Value Proposition

ICO projects often structured their offerings in ways that incentivized early investors with substantial discounts, bonuses, or unique privileges. These tokenomics strategies created a sense of urgency and excitement, encouraging investors to participate during the initial stages to secure the best deals. We analyze how ICO projects strategically designed their token economics to enhance the allure of quick returns, exploring the various mechanisms used to attract a flood of early investments.

The Hype Machine: Marketing and Buzz

Marketing played an essential role in driving the allure of quick profits. ICO projects harnessed the power of social media, influencer endorsements, and online communities to create a sense of anticipation and excitement around their offerings. We explore the tactics deployed by projects to generate hype and build buzz, examining how these strategies exploited investors' desire for rapid returns and drove participation in ICOs.

The Gamification of Investment

In the fast-paced world of ICOs, investing often took on a gamified quality. The speed at which ICOs sold out, the competitive nature of securing tokens, and the potential for overnight gains turned the act of investing into an adrenaline-fueled experience. We delve into how ICOs incorporated gamification elements to heighten the allure of quick returns, transforming investing into an exhilarating and addictive pursuit.

Balancing Risk and Reward

While the allure of quick profits drove many to participate in ICOs, it wasn't without its risks. The volatile nature of the cryptocurrency market and the lack of regulatory oversight meant that potential rewards were accompanied by substantial uncertainty. We explore the fine balance investors faced between the potential for substantial gains and the ever-present risk of losing their investments.

As we continue exploring the captivating stories of ICOs, we'll delve into the deceptive practices that emerged and the impact of spectacular crashes that shattered dreams. By understanding the allure of quick returns, we gain insight into the dynamics that fueled the ICO Mania, shaping its trajectory and leaving a lasting impact on the cryptocurrency landscape.

Chapter 2: The Deceptive Web

Red Flags Ignored: Examine the warning signs and red flags that were overlooked by investors in their pursuit of lucrative opportunities.

In the exuberant rush of the Initial Coin Offering (ICO) Mania, investors found themselves swept up in a whirlwind of innovation and potential profits. However, amidst the excitement, there were subtle indicators and red flags that hinted at the potential risks lurking beneath the surface. This section delves into the warning signs that were often ignored or underestimated by eager investors, shedding light on the psychological and contextual factors that contributed to the overlooking of these red flags.

The Hindsight Bias

Hindsight is often the sharpest lens through which we perceive past events. Many red flags that would later become glaringly obvious were initially brushed aside or overlooked in the fervor of the ICO Mania. We explore the hindsight bias—the tendency to see events as predictable after they've occurred—and how it influenced investors' perceptions of projects that ultimately turned out to be fraudulent or unsustainable.

Echo Chambers and Confirmation Bias

The allure of ICOs was often discussed in online communities and social media platforms where enthusiasts gathered to share insights, opinions, and investment advice. Unfortunately, these spaces sometimes became echo chambers, where confirmation bias reinforced the belief that the projects they favored were infallible. We analyze how echo chambers and confirmation bias played a role in blinding investors to red flags and dissenting opinions.

Pressure to Conform and Participate

In the world of ICOs, participation often carried an air of urgency. Projects frequently set tight timelines for token sales, fostering an atmosphere where investors felt compelled to make quick decisions. This pressure to conform and participate may have led some to overlook red flags in the hope of not missing out on potentially lucrative opportunities. We explore how time constraints influenced investor decision-making and the implications for red flag detection.

Complex Technical Jargon

Whitepapers and project documentation often contained complex technical jargon that posed challenges for non-experts to fully understand. The mystique surrounding blockchain technology and cryptocurrency projects sometimes discouraged potential investors from thoroughly scrutinizing these documents for red flags. We delve into how the use of intricate language may have concealed critical information and contributed to the underestimation of red flags.

Overpromising and Underdelivering

Some ICO projects leveraged grandiose promises to attract investors, even if the feasibility of those promises was questionable. The allure of ambitious visions often led investors to focus on the potential rewards while downplaying the risks associated with overpromising. We examine case studies of projects that overpromised and the factors that influenced investors to ignore the red flags inherent in those claims.

Exaggerated Credentials and Backgrounds

Founders and team members often showcased impressive credentials and backgrounds to instill confidence in their projects. However, not all these claims were verifiable, and some projects resorted to inflating their team's qualifications to gain trust. We explore how investors' tendency to associate expertise with credibility may have led them to overlook inconsistencies or exaggerations that signaled potential red flags.

Navigating the Murky Waters

As we analyze the red flags that were ignored during the ICO Mania, it's important to recognize that the pursuit of lucrative opportunities was driven by a mixture of hope, optimism, and trust. Investors were often navigating unfamiliar territory, and the complex interplay of psychological biases and contextual pressures made it challenging to identify potential pitfalls. In the sections that follow, we'll delve into the deceptive practices employed by fraudulent ICO projects, shedding light on how these schemes exploited the enthusiasm and vulnerabilities of unsuspecting investors. By understanding the warning signs that were missed, we gain a deeper understanding of the dynamics that contributed to the darker aspects of the ICO Mania.

The Art of Deception: Unravel the tactics used by fraudulent ICO projects to create an illusion of legitimacy.

In the midst of the Initial Coin Offering (ICO) Mania, as the cryptocurrency community rallied around innovative projects, a darker underbelly was also at play. Fraudulent ICO projects, armed with elaborate strategies, leveraged the enthusiasm and trust of investors to create an illusion of legitimacy. This section delves into the intricacies of the tactics employed by these malicious actors, unraveling the complex web of deception they wove to cloak their true intentions.

The Mirage of Team Credibility

Fraudulent ICO projects understood the significance of a credible team in instilling trust. Leveraging fabricated profiles and borrowed expertise, they constructed an image of experienced professionals at the helm. We explore how these actors deceived investors by constructing elaborate narratives that showcased a diverse array of skills and backgrounds, often using images and names from stock photos or real professionals unrelated to the project.

Whitepaper Wizardry: The Illusion of Substance

A well-crafted whitepaper was the cornerstone of any ICO, and fraudulent projects capitalized on this. By plagiarizing content from legitimate projects, recycling technical details, and using complex jargon, these actors created the illusion of substance. We examine how the art of deception extended to whitepapers, where seemingly comprehensive documents masked a lack of genuine innovation and execution capability.

Faux Partnerships and Endorsements

The credibility gained from partnerships and endorsements was another tool in the arsenal of deceptive ICO projects. By associating themselves with well-known brands or influencers, they sought to capitalize on the halo effect and the trust that these names carried. We delve into how fraudulent projects fabricated or exaggerated partnerships to create an air of legitimacy that misled even the most discerning investors.

Fabricated Media Coverage

Fraudulent ICOs recognized the power of media coverage in shaping public perception. To create an aura of authenticity, some projects went to great lengths to fabricate news articles, press releases, and reviews that celebrated their supposed achievements. We explore how these actors exploited the ease of online publishing to manipulate public opinion and enhance their illusion of credibility.

Bogus Technical Progress

Legitimate ICO projects often showcased technical development as a sign of progress. Fraudulent projects, aware of this, created the façade of active development by publishing code repositories, issuing updates, and showcasing prototype versions of products. We analyze how these projects masked their lack of substantial progress behind a carefully orchestrated smokescreen of technical activity.

Hijacked Communities and Falsified Engagement

Online communities and social media platforms were pivotal in creating hype around ICO projects. Fraudulent actors infiltrated these spaces, creating fake accounts and bots to mimic enthusiastic engagement and endorsements. We investigate how these deceptive practices manipulated the perceptions of community members, leading to a snowball effect of trust and investment.

The Anatomy of an Illusion

The art of deception was a multi-faceted endeavor that extended beyond a single tactic. Fraudulent ICO projects meticulously orchestrated a symphony of credibility to deceive investors and stakeholders. By weaving together elements of team credibility, technical prowess, partnerships, media coverage, and community engagement, they crafted an elaborate illusion that was difficult to see through.

In the sections that follow, we'll delve into the impact of this deceptive web on investor trust and the broader crypto community. By understanding the tactics employed by fraudulent ICO projects, we gain insight into the vulnerabilities that existed within the ICO Mania and the lessons that continue to shape investor due diligence and skepticism in the cryptocurrency landscape.

The Impact on Investor Trust: Discuss the fallout from deceitful ICOs and how it affected trust within the crypto community.

The rise of the Initial Coin Offering (ICO) Mania brought not only innovation and excitement but also a series of fraudulent schemes that eroded investor trust. As deceitful ICOs unveiled their true colors, the shockwaves reverberated far beyond financial losses. This section delves into the profound impact of these fraudulent endeavors on investor trust and the broader crypto community, examining how the fallout reshaped perceptions and catalyzed a paradigm shift in due diligence and skepticism.

The Trust Deficit

At the heart of investor participation in ICOs lay trust—in the technology, the teams, and the visions presented. The revelation of deceitful ICOs fundamentally shattered this trust, leaving investors feeling betrayed and disillusioned. We explore how this trust deficit created a ripple effect, affecting not only investor sentiment but also the overall credibility of the cryptocurrency industry as a whole.

Erosion of Community Cohesion

The cryptocurrency community was built upon a foundation of shared values, ideals, and visions for a more open and equitable financial future. The exposure of fraudulent ICOs disrupted this sense of unity, fostering suspicion and discord among community members. We examine how the breaches of trust sowed seeds of doubt and division, straining the sense of camaraderie that had characterized the early crypto movement.

The Emotional Toll

Investors who fell victim to fraudulent ICOs experienced not only financial losses but also a deep emotional toll. Dreams of financial freedom and participation in innovative projects were replaced with feelings of betrayal, anger, and regret. We delve into the emotional journey of those affected by deceitful ICOs, highlighting how the aftermath extended beyond financial implications.

The Ripple Effect: Broader Industry Perception

The impact of fraudulent ICOs extended beyond those directly affected; it cast a shadow over the entire cryptocurrency industry. News of scams and rugpulls dominated headlines, creating a narrative that painted the entire industry with a brush of skepticism. We explore how the actions of a few malicious actors cast doubt on the genuine potential of blockchain technology and the projects seeking to leverage it for positive change.

The Call for Due Diligence

As the dust settled, a collective realization emerged: due diligence was not just an option; it was a necessity. Investors, regulators, and industry participants recognized the imperative to scrutinize projects more thoroughly before investing. We analyze how the scars left by deceitful ICOs prompted a renewed focus on research, transparency, and accountability within the cryptocurrency space.

The Birth of Skepticism

The era of fraudulent ICOs gave birth to a new ethos of skepticism—one that encouraged critical inquiry, healthy skepticism, and a demand for verifiable information. This skepticism was not a rejection of innovation but a defense mechanism against future deceit. We explore how the lessons learned from the ICO Mania fundamentally reshaped the way investors approached new projects and opportunities.

Catalyst for Change

While the impact of deceitful ICOs was undeniably negative, it also served as a catalyst for positive change. The scars left by these events prompted industry-wide introspection, leading to initiatives that prioritized investor education, regulatory oversight, and self-policing within the crypto community. We delve into how the fallout from fraudulent ICOs ultimately paved the way for a more mature and accountable ecosystem.

As we progress through this chapter, we'll continue to explore the aftermath of deceitful ICOs, examining the spectacular crashes that shook the community and the efforts to hold fraudulent actors accountable. By understanding the impact on investor trust, we gain a deeper appreciation for the resilience and adaptability of the crypto community in the face of adversity.

Chapter 3: The Spectacular Crashes
From Boom to Bust: Trace the journey of ICO projects that experienced spectacular crashes and sudden collapses.

The meteoric rise of the Initial Coin Offering (ICO) Mania was often followed by dramatic crashes that left investors reeling. While some projects held the promise of revolutionizing industries, their journeys took an abrupt turn as the reality of mismanagement, deception, and unsustainable business models came to light. This section delves into the captivating stories of ICO projects that went from the heights of hype to the depths of failure, tracing their trajectories from boom to bust.

The Frenzy of FOMO

The rapid ascent of many ICO projects was fueled by a potent mix of hype, fear of missing out (FOMO), and irrational exuberance. Investors rushed to contribute, often without conducting thorough due diligence, as they feared being left behind. We examine how the intoxicating cocktail of FOMO contributed to the massive influx of funds into projects that ultimately lacked the substance to deliver on their promises.

The Illusion of Progress

Many ICO projects carefully curated an image of progress, often providing updates, prototypes, and technical advancements to maintain investor confidence. However, behind the scenes, the reality was often starkly different. We explore case studies of projects that projected an illusion of technical advancement while grappling with internal challenges, funding shortages, and insurmountable obstacles.

The Turning Point: Unmasking Deception

As the exuberance of the ICO Mania subsided, cracks in the façade began to emerge. Investigative journalists, community members, and whistleblowers started to reveal discrepancies in whitepapers, exaggerated claims, and even outright fraud. We delve into pivotal moments where the veil of deception was lifted, leaving investors shocked by the vast disparity between the projected visions and the actual state of affairs.

The Fall from Grace

The transition from boom to bust was often swift and brutal. Projects that once captured imaginations suddenly faced a barrage of criticism, legal challenges, and community backlash. We trace the unfolding narrative of these projects as they grappled with the harsh realities of mismanagement, lack of execution, and dwindling investor trust.

Investor Fallout and Financial Losses

The spectacular crashes of ICO projects left a trail of financial devastation in their wake. Investors who had once harbored dreams of lucrative returns found themselves grappling with substantial losses. We examine the stories of individuals and groups affected by these crashes, shedding light on the emotional toll of dashed hopes and shattered dreams.

Repercussions Beyond Financial Loss

The fallout from spectacular crashes wasn't confined to financial losses alone. The broader crypto community felt the reverberations, with trust eroded and skepticism heightened. We delve into how these crashes acted as cautionary tales, prompting industry participants to reevaluate their investment strategies and due diligence practices.

The Aftermath: Lessons Learned

The spectacular crashes served as potent reminders of the risks inherent in the world of ICOs. They highlighted the need for greater accountability, transparency, and regulatory oversight. We explore how these crashes shaped the evolving landscape of the cryptocurrency industry, ushering in a period of introspection, reform, and the adoption of more cautious investment practices.

As we journey further into this chapter, we will continue to explore the repercussions of these crashes, delving into the consequences for investors' financial well-being and emotional resilience. By tracing the trajectories from boom to bust, we gain insights into the vulnerabilities that were exploited by fraudulent projects and the imperative for a more resilient and responsible crypto ecosystem.

Vanished Dreams: Understand the consequences of these failed ICO ventures on investors' financial well-being and emotional resilience.

The euphoria of the Initial Coin Offering (ICO) Mania was often followed by a harsh reality: the sudden collapse of projects that investors had pinned their hopes on. Beyond the financial losses lay a profound impact on individuals' well-being and emotional resilience. This section delves into the stories of investors who saw their dreams of financial freedom and innovation vanish, exploring the tangible and emotional aftermath of these failed ICO ventures.

The Weight of Financial Losses

Investors who participated in ICOs during the Mania were lured by the prospect of substantial returns. The collapse of projects meant not only the loss of invested funds but also the evaporation of the potential profits that had fueled their participation. We delve into the financial burden these losses placed on investors, examining how some faced significant setbacks in their financial goals, investments, and personal finances.

The Emotional Roller Coaster

Investing in ICOs was never just about money; it was about participating in a movement, a vision for a decentralized and innovative future. When these dreams shattered, so did the emotional connections investors had formed with their investments. We explore the emotional roller coaster that investors experienced—ranging from shock, anger, and disbelief to self-blame and frustration.

Nurtured Hopes and High Expectations

The narratives spun by ICO projects often resonated with investors' personal aspirations. Whether it was the promise of democratizing finance, improving supply chains, or revolutionizing industries, these projects tapped into deeply held beliefs. We examine how these nurtured hopes and high expectations made the failure of projects particularly devastating, as they represented not just financial losses, but the loss of a future envisioned.

Strained Relationships and Trust

The pursuit of ICO investments wasn't isolated; it often involved shared goals with family, friends, and fellow enthusiasts. The collapse of projects strained these relationships, as investors grappled with the guilt and responsibility of recommending investments that ultimately failed. We delve into how these broken investments had repercussions beyond the individual, affecting trust and relationships within personal and professional circles.

Navigating Stigma and Self-Blame

Investors who fell victim to failed ICOs often faced stigma and self-blame. The pressure to have made the right investment decisions in a fast-paced and complex landscape weighed heavily on them. We explore how individuals grappled with feelings of embarrassment, self-doubt, and the fear of being judged by peers who hadn't taken part in the ICO frenzy.

Coping Strategies and Resilience

While the aftermath of failed ICOs was undeniably challenging, many investors exhibited remarkable resilience. Some turned to education and self-improvement, while others found solace in support groups and community discussions. We delve into the coping strategies employed by investors to overcome the emotional toll of their losses and navigate the path forward.

The Path to Healing

The process of healing from the emotional scars left by failed ICO investments was multifaceted. It involved acknowledging the losses, seeking professional guidance when needed, and fostering a sense of empowerment and agency. We examine how investors gradually reclaimed their emotional well-being and reconstructed their perspectives on investing and the cryptocurrency ecosystem.

As we continue to explore the consequences of spectacular crashes, we'll delve into the repercussions for the broader crypto space and the insights garnered from these experiences. By understanding the impact on emotional resilience and well-being, we gain a deeper appreciation for the challenges investors faced during the ICO Mania and the lessons that have since influenced the way individuals approach risk and investment decisions in the cryptocurrency landscape.

Repercussions on the Crypto Space: Analyze how the high-profile collapses affected the overall perception of the crypto industry.

The downfall of numerous Initial Coin Offering (ICO) projects during the Mania had far-reaching consequences that extended beyond individual investors. The reverberations of these high-profile collapses echoed throughout the broader crypto space, influencing public perception, regulatory attitudes, and the trajectory of the industry itself. This section delves into how these spectacular crashes cast a shadow over the crypto industry and ushered in a period of reckoning and transformation.

Crisis of Confidence

The dramatic collapses of high-profile ICO projects shook the foundation of investor confidence. The cryptocurrency industry, once heralded as a disruptor of traditional finance, faced scrutiny as fraudulent schemes exposed vulnerabilities and gaps in due diligence. We explore how these collapses eroded public trust and fueled skepticism about the legitimacy of the entire crypto ecosystem.

Media Frenzy and Negative Narratives

The media played a pivotal role in shaping the perception of ICO crashes. The sensational coverage of fraud and deception created a narrative that painted the entire crypto industry with a broad brush of suspicion. We analyze how media narratives influenced public opinion, and how the collective impact of these narratives contributed to a perception of the crypto space as a haven for scams and fraudulent activities.

Regulatory Scrutiny Intensified

The collapse of high-profile ICOs brought regulatory agencies and governments to the forefront. The need to protect investors and maintain market integrity led to heightened regulatory scrutiny. We delve into how the crashes prompted regulators to evaluate the need for stronger oversight, transparency, and investor protection measures within the cryptocurrency industry.

Investor Aversion and Market Impact

The high-profile collapses fostered a sense of investor aversion toward ICOs and riskier investment propositions. As ICO projects imploded, the fear of being burned by fraud or financial loss led many to shy away from the crypto market altogether. We explore how these shifts in investor behavior impacted market dynamics and contributed to the overall market sentiment.

Innovation vs. Risk Perception

The cryptocurrency industry has always been a breeding ground for innovation, driven by the potential for transformative technological breakthroughs. However, the crashes highlighted a stark contrast between innovation and the associated risks. We examine how the emphasis on innovation was counterbalanced by growing concerns about risk and the need for more responsible practices.

Long-Term Implications for the Crypto Ecosystem

The reverberations from the high-profile ICO crashes set the stage for a period of transformation within the crypto ecosystem. Investors, projects, and regulators were compelled to reevaluate their roles and responsibilities. We analyze how the crashes catalyzed discussions about best practices, self-regulation, and a more cautious approach to investment and innovation.

A Paradigm Shift in Perception

While the crashes initially cast a shadow over the crypto space, they also acted as a catalyst for change. The industry was forced to confront its vulnerabilities and address the systemic issues that had allowed fraudulent projects to thrive. We explore how the negative perception resulting from the crashes ultimately became a driving force behind a shift toward greater transparency, accountability, and sustainable growth.

As we proceed through this chapter, we'll continue to delve into the aftermath of high-profile collapses, examining how the crypto industry navigated the challenges posed by these events. By understanding the repercussions on the broader crypto space, we gain insights into the dynamics that shaped its evolution and the lessons that propelled it toward a more mature and resilient future.

Chapter 4: Grasping the Aftermath

Facing the Reality: Witness how investors coped with the aftermath of rugpulls and financial losses.

The aftermath of rugpulls and financial losses from the collapse of Initial Coin Offering (ICO) projects was a period of reckoning for investors who found themselves grappling with the abrupt destruction of their dreams. This section dives into the personal narratives of those who faced the harsh reality of financial losses, exploring their diverse coping mechanisms, emotional journeys, and efforts to regain their footing amidst the wreckage.

Shock and Disbelief

The suddenness of rugpulls and financial losses left investors in a state of shock and disbelief. The realization that projects they had fervently believed in had crumbled undermined not just their investments, but their faith in the cryptocurrency ecosystem. We delve into the initial emotional responses of investors, ranging from disbelief to anger and sadness.

Navigating Emotional Turmoil

The emotional turmoil that followed rugpulls and financial losses was a complex journey. Investors experienced a mix of emotions, including embarrassment, regret, and self-doubt. We explore how individuals grappled with these feelings, and the ways they attempted to process their experiences, whether through seeking support from loved ones, seeking professional guidance, or joining communities of fellow victims.

Coping Mechanisms: Education and Empowerment

As the initial shock subsided, some investors turned to education as a way to regain a sense of control. They embarked on journeys of self-education, learning about blockchain technology, due diligence practices, and the intricacies of investment. We examine how this thirst for knowledge transformed the experiences of these individuals and empowered them to make more informed decisions.

Community Support and Solidarity

Facing the aftermath of rugpulls was a shared experience for many investors. Online forums, social media groups, and support networks became spaces where victims found solace, camaraderie, and validation. We delve into the ways in which community support played a crucial role in alleviating the isolation and stigma associated with financial losses.

The Quest for Accountability

Many investors sought accountability in the wake of rugpulls, aiming to hold fraudulent actors responsible for their actions. Some embarked on legal journeys, while others collaborated with investigative journalists to uncover the truth behind the collapses. We explore how these efforts to seek justice were driven by a desire to prevent others from falling victim to similar schemes.

Rebuilding Financial Resilience

The journey toward rebuilding financial resilience after rugpulls was marked by cautious steps and calculated decisions. Some investors chose to diversify their portfolios, while others engaged in more rigorous due diligence. We delve into the strategies employed to regain financial stability and the lessons that emerged from the process.

Redefining Success and Goals

For many investors, rugpulls and financial losses prompted a reevaluation of their definitions of success and goals. The pursuit of quick profits gave way to a more tempered approach that valued sustainability, transparency, and long-term growth. We explore how these shifts in perspective shaped the way investors engaged with the crypto industry moving forward.

The Road to Healing

Over time, investors who faced the aftermath of rugpulls embarked on a journey of healing and renewal. The scars of financial losses remained, but many found ways to rebuild their lives and their relationships with the crypto space. We examine how individuals emerged from the rubble of rugpulls with a newfound sense of resilience, wisdom, and cautious optimism.

As we move forward in this chapter, we'll continue to explore the efforts to hold fraudulent ICO operators accountable and the role of social media in promoting and exposing ICO scams. By understanding the ways in which investors coped with the aftermath of rugpulls, we gain insight into the remarkable capacity for growth and adaptation that emerged from the challenges of the ICO Mania.

Legal Battles: Explore the legal battles and efforts to hold fraudulent ICO operators accountable.

The unraveling of fraudulent Initial Coin Offering (ICO) projects wasn't just a matter of financial loss; it was a breach of trust and the foundation of the cryptocurrency industry itself. As investors grappled with the aftermath, many sought justice through legal means, aiming to hold deceitful operators accountable for their actions. This section delves into the complex landscape of legal battles that emerged in the wake of ICO collapses, highlighting the challenges, successes, and lessons learned in the pursuit of accountability.

The Legal Landscape: Complex and Evolving

Navigating the legal terrain surrounding fraudulent ICOs was a daunting task. The lack of standardized regulations and the international nature of these schemes posed challenges in determining jurisdiction, applicable laws, and legal avenues for recourse. We explore how the absence of clear regulatory frameworks affected the ability to pursue legal action effectively.

Investor Rights and Class Actions

As financial losses mounted, some investors united in their pursuit of justice through class-action lawsuits. These efforts aimed to pool resources, share information, and increase the collective impact of legal action against deceitful ICO operators. We examine how class actions empowered investors and the potential they held in holding accountable those who exploited their trust.

Building the Case: Uncovering Evidence

Mounting a legal battle required a substantial amount of evidence to establish wrongdoing. Investors, legal teams, and investigative journalists collaborated to piece together the puzzle of deceit, uncovering whitepaper discrepancies, fabricated partnerships, and misrepresented achievements. We delve into how the gathering of evidence was critical in building strong cases against fraudulent operators.

Challenges and Legal Complexities

Legal battles against fraudulent ICO operators were not without obstacles. Many operators employed tactics to obfuscate their identities, locations, and financial transactions. The anonymity afforded by blockchain technology presented unique challenges in identifying responsible parties and tracing misappropriated funds. We analyze the legal complexities that arose in the pursuit of accountability.

Jurisdictional Dilemmas and Cross-Border Implications

The international nature of the cryptocurrency industry added layers of complexity to legal battles. Fraudulent operators often operated across borders, making it difficult to determine which jurisdiction's laws applied. We explore the jurisdictional dilemmas that arose and the efforts to collaborate between legal systems to effectively address transnational fraud.

Settlements, Recovery, and Restitution

Some legal battles against fraudulent ICOs culminated in settlements, where operators agreed to compensate affected investors. These settlements offered a path to recovery and restitution for victims. We delve into the negotiations, challenges, and impact of settlements on the affected parties and the broader crypto community.

Preventing Recurrence: Deterrence and Precedent

Legal battles against fraudulent ICOs had broader implications beyond individual cases. Successful prosecutions and judgments established precedent and served as a deterrent to future malicious actors. We explore how these legal battles played a role in shaping the crypto industry's response to fraudulent schemes and in setting expectations for accountability.

Lessons Learned and Moving Forward

The legal battles against deceitful ICO operators provided insights into the resilience and adaptability of investors in the face of adversity. They also highlighted the need for greater regulatory clarity, investor education, and due diligence practices. As we continue to explore the role of legal battles in grasping the aftermath, we'll delve into the ways social media played a role in both promoting and exposing ICO scams, shedding light on the complexities of the evolving crypto landscape.

The Role of Social Media: Discuss how social media platforms played a role in both promoting and exposing ICO scams.

The rise of the Initial Coin Offering (ICO) Mania was accompanied by a surge in social media engagement, creating an environment that was both conducive to rapid dissemination of information and vulnerable to manipulation. This section delves into the complex interplay between social media platforms, the promotion of ICO scams, and the pivotal role they played in uncovering deceitful practices, highlighting the power of these digital landscapes in shaping investor perceptions and exposing fraudulent schemes.

The Frenzy of Hype and Hype Cycles

Social media platforms became breeding grounds for ICO hype, with projects leveraging these platforms to build momentum, attract investors, and generate excitement. We explore how the virality of posts, tweets, and online discussions created hype cycles, often leading to rapid surges in investment before the true nature of projects was fully understood.

The Amplification Effect

The reach of social media platforms extended far beyond traditional communication channels, allowing projects to bypass traditional gatekeepers and communicate directly with potential investors. However, this unfiltered communication also created an environment ripe for manipulation. We delve into how the amplification effect of social media magnified both the allure and the risks of ICO investments.

Promotion and Shilling: The Dark Side of Influence

While social media platforms provided opportunities for legitimate projects to engage with their communities, they also facilitated the spread of misinformation and fraudulent schemes. Individuals with vested interests engaged in "shilling," promoting projects for personal gain while misleading followers. We explore how this manipulation of influence distorted the landscape of ICO investments.

Social Proof and FOMO

The concept of social proof played a pivotal role in shaping investor behavior. Positive endorsements, influential figures, and an abundance of online enthusiasm created an illusion of credibility that fueled the fear of missing out (FOMO). We examine how the mechanics of social media contributed to the rapid spread of these narratives and the decisions they influenced.

Exposing Deceit: The Power of Crowdsourced Investigation

Social media platforms were also instrumental in exposing deceitful ICO projects. Online communities, vigilant investors, and investigative journalists leveraged these platforms to share information, uncover red flags, and collaboratively scrutinize projects. We delve into case studies of how these crowdsourced investigations played a pivotal role in unmasking fraud and holding fraudulent operators accountable.

The Challenge of Discernment

The rapid pace of information dissemination on social media platforms presented challenges for investors trying to separate fact from fiction. The allure of quick profits often clouded judgment, making it difficult to critically evaluate projects amidst the noise. We explore the complexities investors faced in discerning between genuine opportunities and fraudulent schemes.

The Role of Regulation and Platform Responsibility

The impact of social media platforms on ICO promotion and exposure led to discussions about regulation and platform responsibility. Some argued for increased oversight and accountability to mitigate the risks of spreading fraudulent information. We examine the ongoing debates about the role that social media platforms should play in preventing the dissemination of fraudulent content.

A Double-Edged Sword: Looking Ahead

As we navigate the evolving landscape of cryptocurrency, social media platforms remain a double-edged sword, simultaneously enabling innovation, education, and communication while also posing risks of manipulation, misinformation, and fraud. By understanding the role of social media in promoting and exposing ICO scams, we gain insight into the challenges and opportunities that these platforms present in a digitally connected world.

Continuing through this chapter, we'll delve into the efforts to strengthen due diligence processes and self-regulation within the crypto community, exploring how the lessons learned from the ICO Mania influenced the industry's path toward greater maturity and resilience.

Chapter 5: Rebuilding Trust and Credibility

Strengthening Due Diligence: Understand how the crypto community enhanced due diligence processes to avoid future scams.

The collapse of numerous Initial Coin Offering (ICO) projects during the Mania shook the foundations of trust within the cryptocurrency community. In response, participants in the ecosystem recognized the urgency of bolstering due diligence practices to prevent future scams. This section delves into the steps taken by the crypto community to refine their approach to project assessment, investment decisions, and risk mitigation, highlighting the collaborative efforts to create a more resilient and informed landscape.

Learning from Mistakes: The Imperative for Due Diligence

The aftermath of ICO rugpulls underscored the importance of thorough due diligence. Investors, projects, and regulatory bodies acknowledged that the pursuit of innovation couldn't come at the cost of overlooking essential checks and balances. We explore how the painful lessons from the Mania instilled a renewed commitment to due diligence across the crypto community.

Informed Investor Education

One of the cornerstones of enhanced due diligence was informed investor education. Industry participants recognized that educated investors were more likely to make sound decisions and avoid falling prey to scams. We delve into initiatives that aimed to educate individuals about blockchain technology, investment principles, and the warning signs of fraudulent projects.

Transparency as a Standard

The lack of transparency had been a hallmark of deceitful ICO projects. To counter this, projects and organizations began embracing transparency as a standard practice. We examine how projects sought to demonstrate transparency by sharing their code repositories, technical progress, team credentials, and financial information to build trust with potential investors.

Independent Audits and Reviews

To verify the legitimacy of ICO projects, the crypto community turned to independent audits and reviews. These external assessments provided a level of validation that helped investors make more informed decisions. We explore the rise of independent auditing firms and how their evaluations influenced investor perceptions of project credibility.

Community Engagement and Feedback

The crypto community recognized the value of engaging the collective wisdom of its members. Online communities, forums, and social media platforms became spaces for due diligence collaboration, enabling investors to share insights, ask questions, and collectively assess the legitimacy of projects. We delve into how community feedback played a role in shaping investor perspectives.

Investor Empowerment: Comprehensive Research

Enhanced due diligence extended beyond a checklist of technical and financial factors. Investors were encouraged to conduct comprehensive research, including understanding the project's technology, market fit, competitive landscape, and potential challenges. We examine how this holistic approach empowered investors to make well-rounded assessments.

Refining Investment Practices

The shift toward enhanced due diligence led to a refinement of investment practices. Investors began to adopt a more cautious and analytical approach, diversifying portfolios, and being discerning about where they placed their funds. We explore how the experience of rugpulls prompted a more mature and measured investment behavior.

Regulatory Support and Industry Standards

Regulators acknowledged the importance of due diligence and issued guidelines to promote responsible practices. These standards provided a framework for evaluating ICO projects and set expectations for transparency, disclosure, and investor protection. We delve into how regulatory support complemented community-driven efforts to strengthen due diligence.

Evolving Ecosystem, Evolving Due Diligence

As the cryptocurrency ecosystem continued to evolve, due diligence practices evolved alongside it. The lessons learned from the ICO Mania contributed to a culture of vigilance and skepticism that permeated investment decisions, project assessments, and industry discourse. By understanding the ways in which the crypto community enhanced due diligence processes, we gain insights into the measures taken to prevent future scams and rebuild trust within the ecosystem.

Continuing through this chapter, we'll explore the self-regulation initiatives taken by the industry to protect investors and discuss projects that survived rugpull accusations and successfully rebuilt their reputation, offering hope for a more resilient crypto future.

Self-Regulation Initiatives: Explore the measures taken by the industry to self-regulate and protect investors.

In the wake of the ICO Mania's fallout, the cryptocurrency industry recognized the need for proactive self-regulation to restore investor trust and establish a more secure and transparent environment. This section delves into the various self-regulation initiatives that emerged within the industry, highlighting the collaborative efforts to set standards, enforce best practices, and safeguard the interests of investors and participants.

The Call for Accountability

The collapse of ICO projects revealed the absence of a comprehensive regulatory framework, prompting the crypto community to take matters into its own hands. We explore how the call for accountability led to the formation of self-regulation initiatives aimed at addressing the deficiencies in project assessment, disclosure, and governance.

Establishing Best Practices and Standards

Self-regulation initiatives sought to define best practices and standards that projects could voluntarily adhere to. These standards encompassed transparency in project development, team credentials, code audits, and clear communication with investors. We delve into how the establishment of these benchmarks aimed to enhance credibility and mitigate risks.

Code of Ethics and Conduct

To promote integrity and responsible behavior, some industry associations developed codes of ethics and conduct for ICO projects and participants. These codes outlined principles of transparency, honesty, and commitment to investor protection. We examine how these codes aimed to foster a culture of responsibility and accountability.

Platform Due Diligence and Listings

Cryptocurrency exchanges also recognized the need for self-regulation in listing tokens and coins. Many exchanges implemented due diligence processes to assess the legitimacy of projects before listing them. We explore how these initiatives aimed to provide a level of assurance to investors and prevent the propagation of fraudulent projects.

Third-Party Verification and Audits

To bolster investor confidence, self-regulation initiatives encouraged projects to undergo third-party verification and audits. These external assessments provided independent evaluations of project claims, technologies, and financials. We delve into how third-party verification became a cornerstone of self-regulation efforts.

Educational Initiatives: Empowering Investors

Self-regulation extended beyond projects and encompassed education for investors. The industry recognized the importance of arming investors with the knowledge and tools needed to navigate the complex crypto landscape. We explore how educational initiatives aimed to empower individuals to make informed investment decisions.

Enforcement Mechanisms and Consequences

Effective self-regulation required mechanisms for enforcement and consequences for non-compliance. Some industry associations implemented mechanisms to report fraudulent projects, leading to their expulsion from the community. We delve into the challenges of enforcing self-regulation and the role of the community in holding projects accountable.

Collaboration and Industry Unity

Self-regulation initiatives hinged on collaboration among industry participants. Competing projects, exchanges, investors, and regulatory bodies came together to define and enforce common standards. We examine how this spirit of collaboration led to greater unity within the industry and facilitated a shared commitment to safeguarding the crypto ecosystem.

Balancing Self-Regulation and Innovation

While self-regulation aimed to protect investors and prevent scams, it also had to strike a balance with innovation and entrepreneurial freedom. We explore the challenges of creating a regulatory framework that fosters responsible growth while avoiding stifling innovation.

Charting the Path Forward

The self-regulation initiatives undertaken by the cryptocurrency industry marked a significant step toward rebuilding trust and credibility. By examining these efforts, we gain insight into the industry's commitment to accountability, transparency, and investor protection. As we move through this chapter, we'll further explore projects that survived rugpull accusations and emerged stronger, contributing to the industry's resilience and evolution.

The Road to Recovery: Learn about projects that survived rugpull accusations and rebuilt their reputation.

The tumultuous era of the Initial Coin Offering (ICO) Mania left a trail of financial wreckage and shattered dreams, but it also showcased the resilience of some projects that weathered the storm and emerged stronger. This section delves into the journeys of projects that faced rugpull accusations, navigated the challenges of rebuilding trust, and ultimately managed to restore their reputation within the crypto community.

The Aftermath: Navigating Accusations

For projects accused of rugpulling or engaging in fraudulent activities, the immediate aftermath was marked by skepticism, backlash, and loss of investor confidence. We explore how projects reacted to the accusations, the steps they took to address concerns, and their initial strategies for mitigating reputational damage.

Transparency as a Cornerstone

Surviving rugpull accusations often required an unwavering commitment to transparency. Projects that recognized the power of open communication with their community were better equipped to rebuild trust. We delve into case studies of how projects laid bare their operations, development progress, and financials in order to demonstrate their commitment to honesty and accountability.

Community Engagement and Redemption

Projects that managed to rebuild their reputation engaged with their community in a process of redemption. Open forums, regular updates, and direct interactions with investors were vital in demonstrating sincerity and regaining trust. We examine how these initiatives helped to turn skepticism into support and contribute to the project's credibility.

Audit and Verification

Rebuilding reputation necessitated more than just words; it required action. Some projects subjected themselves to independent audits and third-party verification to validate their claims and technology. We explore how these external assessments played a role in assuring investors of the project's authenticity.

Learning from Mistakes: Evolution of Governance

The experience of facing rugpull accusations prompted some projects to reflect on their governance structures. Lessons learned from the past informed changes to decision-making processes, team accountability, and the involvement of community members. We delve into how these adjustments contributed to a more mature and responsible project.

Adapting to Market Realities

Projects that survived the storm also demonstrated adaptability. They recognized the need to adapt to changing market conditions, pivot their strategies, and prove their worth in a competitive landscape. We examine how flexibility and resilience played a role in a project's ability to recover and thrive.

Re-Establishing Credibility with Partners

Rebuilding reputation extended beyond the community to partners, exchanges, and potential collaborators. Projects needed to restore their credibility within the broader crypto ecosystem in order to secure partnerships and listing opportunities. We explore how projects navigated these challenges and negotiated new alliances.

Ongoing Efforts: Sustaining Trust

Rebuilding reputation was not a one-time endeavor; it required sustained efforts to maintain transparency, community engagement, and operational integrity. Projects that successfully weathered the storm continued to uphold these principles even after their reputation had been restored. We examine how ongoing efforts contributed to long-term trust.

The Impact on the Industry

The journeys of projects that survived rugpull accusations had a broader impact on the crypto industry. Their experiences provided valuable lessons for other projects, investors, and the community at large. By examining these stories, we gain insights into the qualities and strategies that foster resilience, redemption, and a renewed commitment to ethical practices.

Continuing through this chapter, we'll delve into how regulatory responses shaped the industry landscape and explore the challenges of striking a balance between regulation and innovation. These narratives collectively shed light on the evolution of the crypto industry as it emerged from the shadows of the ICO Mania, incorporating lessons learned into a more mature and responsible ecosystem.

Chapter 6: Regulatory Waves

Regulatory Responses: Examine how governments and financial regulators responded to the ICO boom and the rising concerns about investor protection.

The meteoric rise of the Initial Coin Offering (ICO) Mania sent shockwaves through the global financial landscape, raising urgent questions about investor protection, market integrity, and regulatory oversight. In this section, we delve into the diverse responses of governments and financial regulators around the world as they grappled with the challenges posed by the ICO boom, navigating the delicate balance between fostering innovation and safeguarding investors.

The Regulatory Landscape Pre-ICO Mania

Before the ICO Mania, the regulatory landscape for cryptocurrencies was nascent and often fragmented. We provide an overview of the regulatory climate leading up to the boom and how the lack of standardized frameworks left room for unscrupulous actors to exploit the system.

Rising Concerns: Red Flags and Vulnerabilities

As ICOs gained prominence, red flags and vulnerabilities became increasingly apparent. The lack of investor protection, the prevalence of fraudulent schemes, and the potential for financial instability triggered alarm among regulators. We explore the factors that prompted regulatory authorities to take action.

Regulatory Divergence: Global Approaches

Different countries responded to the ICO Mania with a range of regulatory approaches. Some embraced ICOs as a means of fostering innovation, while others issued warnings and imposed restrictions. We analyze how jurisdictions like the United States, China, Switzerland, and Japan varied in their responses to the ICO frenzy.

Securities Regulation and Howey Test

A significant regulatory challenge was determining whether ICO tokens were considered securities and thus subject to existing securities regulations. We delve into the Howey Test, a legal framework used to assess whether an investment qualifies as a security, and how its application affected ICO classification.

SEC Enforcement Actions: Establishing Precedent

The U.S. Securities and Exchange Commission (SEC) played a prominent role in shaping the regulatory response to ICOs. We examine the landmark enforcement actions taken by the SEC against fraudulent ICOs, the impact on the industry, and how these actions set a precedent for future regulatory measures.

Regulatory Warnings and Guidance

As concerns about investor protection escalated, regulatory authorities issued warnings and guidance to educate investors about the risks associated with ICO investments. We explore how these initiatives aimed to empower individuals to make informed decisions while fostering a greater understanding of potential pitfalls.

Creating ICO Frameworks: Switzerland and Singapore

Certain countries chose to create regulatory frameworks specifically tailored to ICOs. Switzerland and Singapore, for instance, embraced ICOs under certain conditions and established guidelines to balance innovation with investor protection. We analyze these frameworks and their effectiveness.

Initial Coin Offering Regulations: Striking the Balance

Regulators faced the challenge of striking a balance between enabling innovation and protecting investors. We examine how various regulatory measures aimed to achieve this equilibrium, including disclosure requirements, investor accreditation, and limitations on fundraising amounts.

The Ripple Effect: Impact on ICO Landscape

The regulatory responses to the ICO Mania had a ripple effect on the broader ICO landscape. Projects reconsidered their strategies, investors evaluated risk factors more rigorously, and the industry as a whole matured in response to the changing regulatory environment. We explore how regulatory actions catalyzed these shifts.

Unintended Consequences and Regulatory Challenges

While regulatory efforts sought to curb fraudulent activities, they also presented challenges. Over-regulation risked stifling innovation and driving legitimate projects offshore. We delve into the unintended consequences of certain regulatory measures and the ongoing debates within the crypto community.

Lessons Learned and Future Outlook

By examining the regulatory responses to the ICO boom, we gain insight into the industry's evolution and the lessons learned about investor protection, responsible innovation, and the need for international cooperation. As we move forward in this chapter, we'll compare international perspectives on ICO regulation and explore the delicate balance of implementing regulations without stifling growth and creativity.

International Perspectives: Compare the regulatory approaches in different countries and their impact on the global crypto landscape.

The ICO Mania catapulted cryptocurrencies and blockchain technology onto the global stage, prompting governments and regulators worldwide to grapple with the challenges and opportunities presented by this emerging industry. In this section, we delve into the diverse regulatory approaches taken by different countries, examining their motivations, strategies, and the far-reaching implications for the global crypto landscape.

A Global Phenomenon: ICOs and Regulatory Diversity

The international nature of cryptocurrencies meant that regulatory responses varied significantly from one country to another. We explore how the ICO Mania created a global phenomenon that demanded localized regulatory solutions, leading to a tapestry of different approaches.

United States: Navigating the Balance

The United States, as a major player in the crypto space, struggled to strike a balance between fostering innovation and protecting investors. We analyze how regulatory agencies like the SEC responded to ICOs, the classification of tokens as securities, and the subsequent impact on the ICO landscape.

China: Swift Restrictions and the Blanket Ban

China took a firm stance on ICOs, imposing an outright ban on token sales and exchanges. We delve into China's motivations for these restrictions, the impact on the global market, and the subsequent migration of Chinese projects to more accommodating jurisdictions.

Switzerland: The Crypto Valley Experiment

Switzerland emerged as a hotspot for blockchain innovation and ICOs, creating a favorable regulatory environment through a combination of guidelines and principles. We examine how the "Crypto Valley" in Zug attracted projects and investment, and the lessons learned from this experiment in regulation.

Singapore: Nurturing Innovation with Pragmatism

Singapore adopted a pragmatic approach to ICOs, providing clarity on regulatory expectations while allowing room for innovation. We explore how Singapore's framework balanced investor protection with the need to foster a vibrant crypto ecosystem.

Japan: Licensing and Consumer Protection

Japan introduced a licensing framework for cryptocurrency exchanges and embraced self-regulation, aiming to ensure consumer protection and market integrity.

We analyze the impact of these measures on the Japanese crypto landscape and how they influenced global trends.

European Union: Collaborative Regulation

The European Union (EU) grappled with harmonizing regulations across member states. We delve into the EU's efforts to create a unified approach to ICOs and crypto assets, the development of the MiCA proposal, and the potential implications for the broader crypto ecosystem.

Australia: Regulatory Sandboxes and Innovation

Australia leveraged regulatory sandboxes to facilitate innovation while maintaining investor protection. We examine how this approach provided a controlled environment for testing new ideas and fostering collaboration between regulators and industry participants.

Global Implications: Competition and Innovation

The regulatory diversity across countries led to competition for talent, projects, and investment. We explore how these variations in regulatory approaches sparked innovation as projects sought out favorable jurisdictions and regulators vied for their share of the emerging crypto landscape.

Challenges of Cross-Border Activities

The decentralized nature of cryptocurrencies created challenges for regulators trying to oversee cross-border activities. We analyze the complexities of regulating global projects, the potential for regulatory arbitrage, and the efforts to create international cooperation frameworks.

Future Harmonization: Prospects and Challenges

The disparate regulatory approaches taken by different countries raise questions about the future harmonization of crypto regulations. We examine the challenges and prospects of achieving international cooperation, the role of forums like the Financial Action Task Force (FATF), and the potential for regulatory convergence.

Impact on Industry Evolution: Lessons and Future Direction

By comparing the regulatory approaches of different countries, we gain insights into how these strategies shaped the global crypto landscape. As we navigate through this chapter, we'll delve into the challenges of finding the balance between regulation and innovation and the potential for the crypto industry to move forward with a more harmonized and coherent regulatory framework.

Striking a Balance: Discuss the challenges of implementing regulations without stifling innovation and growth.

The emergence of the Initial Coin Offering (ICO) Mania cast a spotlight on the regulatory dilemmas faced by governments and financial authorities worldwide. Balancing the need for investor protection with fostering innovation posed a complex challenge. In this section, we explore the delicate equilibrium regulators sought to achieve, the tensions that arose between regulation and innovation, and the ongoing debates about finding the right path forward.

Regulation vs. Innovation: The Dilemma

The ICO Mania highlighted the tension between regulatory oversight and the burgeoning potential of blockchain technology and cryptocurrencies. We delve into how regulatory approaches varied across countries and the overarching dilemma of curbing risks without stifling innovation.

Encouraging Entrepreneurship: The Innovation Imperative

Innovation has been a driving force behind the crypto industry's growth. We examine how regulators navigated the fine line between imposing restrictions and nurturing an environment where entrepreneurs could innovate freely.

Inhibiting Investment: The Risk of Over-Regulation

Striking the right balance meant avoiding over-regulation that could hinder investment and the development of groundbreaking technologies. We explore how an excess of regulatory constraints could lead to a stifling of capital flow and a missed opportunity for economic growth.

Regulatory Uncertainty: Impact on Investment and Development

The lack of regulatory clarity often resulted in uncertainty for projects and investors. We analyze how this uncertainty could deter investment, hinder project development, and create an environment where projects chose to operate in jurisdictions with clearer guidelines.

Innovative Solutions: Regulatory Sandboxes and Pilot Programs

Regulatory sandboxes and pilot programs emerged as innovative solutions to bridge the gap between regulation and innovation. We explore how these controlled environments allowed projects to test their ideas while regulators gathered insights for crafting effective regulations.

Investor Education and Protection: A Prerequisite for Innovation

Robust investor protection was a cornerstone of balanced regulation. We delve into how educating investors about risks, empowering them with knowledge, and enhancing transparency within the industry contributed to a healthier ecosystem.

Industry Collaboration: Regulators and Stakeholders Unite

Striking the balance required collaboration between regulators, industry participants, and other stakeholders. We examine how forums, working groups, and industry associations played a role in facilitating communication and shaping regulatory strategies.

Regulation as a Catalyst for Growth: Market Maturation

Despite its challenges, regulation also served as a catalyst for market maturation. We explore how well-defined regulations provided clarity for projects, increased investor confidence, and contributed to a more stable and credible ecosystem.

The Crypto Paradox: Decentralization vs. Regulation

The decentralized nature of cryptocurrencies added a layer of complexity to the regulatory challenge. We analyze the paradox between decentralized ideals and the need for regulatory oversight, and how the industry grappled with this tension.

Future Directions: The Evolving Regulatory Landscape

As the crypto industry continues to evolve, the challenge of striking a balance between regulation and innovation persists. We examine the ongoing debates about the role of governments, the potential for global regulatory standards, and the need for flexible regulations that adapt to the dynamic nature of the crypto space.

A More Resilient Future: Integrating Lessons Learned

By exploring the challenges of implementing regulations without stifling innovation, we gain insight into the dynamic forces shaping the crypto industry's evolution. As we proceed through this chapter, we'll analyze the lasting impact of the ICO Mania on the crypto ecosystem and how the lessons learned are shaping the industry's journey toward a more mature and sustainable future.

Chapter 7: Evolving Landscape

Shifting Paradigms: Reflect on how the ICO boom and its aftermath influenced the evolution of the crypto space.

The Initial Coin Offering (ICO) Mania left an indelible mark on the cryptocurrency landscape, reshaping perceptions, practices, and priorities within the industry. In this section, we delve into the profound ways in which the ICO boom and its aftermath propelled the crypto space into a new era, redefining its trajectory and catalyzing transformative shifts.

Redefining Funding Models: Beyond ICOs

The ICO Mania brought ICOs into the limelight as a fundraising mechanism, but also exposed their vulnerabilities. We explore how the experience prompted the exploration of alternative funding models such as Security Token Offerings (STOs), Initial Exchange Offerings (IEOs), and Decentralized Finance (DeFi) protocols.

Investor Maturity: From FOMO to Due Diligence

The era of FOMO (Fear of Missing Out) that characterized the ICO Mania gave way to a more mature investor approach. We analyze how investors transitioned from hasty investments driven by hype to more thorough due diligence, informed by the lessons learned from rugpulls.

Rise of Institutional Interest: A New Wave of Participation

Institutional interest in cryptocurrencies gained momentum as the industry matured. We delve into how the ICO boom's aftermath influenced institutions' perception of cryptocurrencies as investable assets and the impact of their increased participation on the market.

From Speculation to Utility: Focus on Use Cases

The ICO Mania's speculative frenzy eventually led to a greater emphasis on real-world use cases. We explore how projects shifted their focus from lofty promises to delivering tangible solutions that addressed actual problems and showcased the potential of blockchain technology.

Governance Evolution: Lessons from ICO Failures

Governance mechanisms within blockchain projects were refined in response to the ICO Mania's failures. We examine how projects incorporated better decision-making structures, community involvement, and transparency, drawing from the experiences of those that faced rugpull accusations.

Regulatory Maturity: The Road to Clarity

The ICO Mania highlighted regulatory challenges and ambiguities. We explore how the industry's experiences influenced regulatory developments, leading to a more defined framework for cryptocurrencies, token offerings, and exchanges.

Decentralization Resilience: Lessons from Centralization

Centralized practices within ICO projects exposed vulnerabilities. We analyze how this experience led to a renewed commitment to decentralization, and the development of projects that prioritize community governance and open participation.

Technology Evolution: Beyond the Hype

The ICO Mania's association with exaggerated promises led to a push for substantive technological progress. We delve into how projects sought to differentiate themselves through genuine advancements in technology, fostering a more credible and resilient ecosystem.

The Maturing Community: Education and Collaboration

The crypto community evolved from being solely driven by speculative interests to becoming more educated and collaborative. We examine how the lessons learned from ICO rugpulls led to a community that values knowledge, collaboration, and responsible investment.

Legacy of Innovation: Paving the Way Forward

The ICO boom's legacy extended beyond the hype and subsequent challenges. We explore how the period's innovation laid the foundation for blockchain projects, platforms, and technologies that continue to drive advancements in fields ranging from finance to supply chain management.

Looking Ahead: A More Resilient Future

Reflecting on the ICO boom's influence, we gain insights into the crypto space's transformation into a more resilient and informed industry. As we continue through this chapter, we'll delve into the lasting impact of the ICO Mania on the crypto ecosystem, explore its legacy, and consider the promising journey ahead.

Lessons Learned: Summarize the crucial lessons and insights gained from the era of ICO rugpulls.

The era of the Initial Coin Offering (ICO) Mania was marked by unprecedented excitement and disillusionment, as well as the unraveling of rugpulls that left a lasting impact on the cryptocurrency industry. In this section, we distill the invaluable lessons and insights that emerged from this tumultuous period, shaping the industry's evolution and fostering a more mature, resilient, and responsible ecosystem.

Investor Vigilance: Due Diligence and Skepticism

One of the most vital lessons was the need for investors to exercise due diligence and skepticism. We explore how the rugpulls highlighted the risks of blind investment, prompting a shift towards informed decision-making and thorough project research.

Transparency as a Pillar of Trust

Transparency emerged as a cornerstone of trust between projects and investors. We delve into how the lack of transparency in some rugpull incidents eroded confidence and how the industry responded with a renewed emphasis on open communication and disclosure.

Risk Management: Diversification and Rationality

Rugpulls underscored the importance of risk management in investment strategies. We examine how investors learned to diversify their portfolios, manage risk exposure, and make rational choices based on thorough analysis rather than emotion.

Project Accountability: Governance and Responsibility

The accountability of projects was brought into sharp focus by rugpull incidents. We analyze how projects began adopting improved governance structures, clearer roadmaps, and mechanisms for accountability to their community.

Educating the Community: Knowledge Over Hype

The ICO Mania exposed the dangers of investing based on hype rather than knowledge. We explore how the industry pivoted to emphasize education, creating resources and platforms to equip individuals with the knowledge needed to navigate the complex crypto landscape.

Regulation's Role: Balancing Innovation and Protection

Regulatory responses to rugpulls provided insight into the delicate balance between innovation and protection. We delve into how regulatory measures aimed at curbing fraud and protecting investors were formulated while avoiding stifling the potential of the industry.

Technology's Value: Substance Over Speculation

The ICO boom spotlighted the need for substantive technological progress over speculative promises. We examine how projects learned that genuine advancements in technology were essential for credibility and long-term success.

Community Empowerment: Collaborative Growth

Rugpulls highlighted the importance of strong community involvement. We explore how projects shifted towards decentralization, community governance, and direct participation, empowering the community to have a say in project directions.

Global Collaboration: Lessons Beyond Borders

The lessons learned from rugpulls transcended borders, prompting collaboration among projects, regulators, and industry players worldwide. We delve into how global forums, working groups, and initiatives sought to share insights and best practices.

Building Trust: From Fragility to Resilience

Rugpulls shattered trust in the industry but also propelled its evolution toward greater resilience. We analyze how the industry transformed from fragility to a more responsible, mature, and trustworthy ecosystem.

A New Era: Applying the Lessons

As we reflect on the lessons learned from the era of ICO rugpulls, we recognize the profound impact of these experiences on shaping the crypto industry's trajectory. Moving forward through this chapter, we'll delve into the lasting legacy of the ICO Mania and its influence on the road ahead, where innovation, collaboration, and responsibility stand as guiding principles for a more sustainable future.

Embracing the Future: Look forward to a more mature and resilient crypto industry that incorporates the learnings from its past.

The crypto industry's journey through the Initial Coin Offering (ICO) Mania and its aftermath has been one of discovery, challenges, and evolution. In this section, we cast our gaze toward the future, envisioning a crypto industry that has absorbed the crucial lessons from its past to create a more mature, resilient, and responsible ecosystem.

Balancing Innovation and Responsibility

The future of the crypto industry rests on the ability to strike a harmonious balance between innovation and responsibility. We explore how projects can maintain a culture of innovation while adhering to best practices, governance, and transparency.

Investor Empowerment: Educating for Success

Investor empowerment is key to a thriving crypto ecosystem. We examine how educational initiatives, resources, and platforms can equip investors with the knowledge needed to navigate risks, make informed decisions, and actively contribute to the industry's growth.

Transparency as a Standard: Trust Through Openness

Transparency remains a linchpin of trust-building. We delve into how projects can adopt transparency as a standard practice, sharing their progress, financials, and decisions openly to foster a sense of trust within the community.

Technology Evolution: Realizing the Potential

The future holds immense potential for blockchain technology beyond speculation. We explore how advancements in scalability, interoperability, security, and user experience will drive the evolution of projects and platforms.

Community-Led Governance: Empowering Decision-Making

Decentralized governance models will play a pivotal role in the future of the industry. We analyze how projects can empower their communities to actively participate in decision-making, fostering a sense of ownership and alignment with project goals.

Global Regulatory Harmonization: Cooperation for Clarity

The lessons from ICO rugpulls will influence the trajectory of regulatory frameworks. We examine the prospects of global regulatory harmonization, enabling a cohesive approach that balances investor protection and innovation across borders.

Institutional Integration: Fostering Mainstream Adoption

Institutions' growing interest in cryptocurrencies will shape the future landscape. We delve into how projects can prepare for institutional integration, compliance, and the potential for greater mainstream adoption.

Responsible Marketing and Communication: Ethical Promotion

Marketing practices will undergo transformation as the industry matures. We explore how projects can market responsibly, avoiding exaggerated claims and embracing authenticity in their communication.

Building Resilience Against Manipulation: Lessons from Rugpulls

The experiences of the ICO Mania offer a roadmap for guarding against manipulation and rugpulls. We analyze how projects can integrate security audits, community vigilance, and responsible leadership to build resilience.

Environmental Responsibility: Sustainability in Focus

The industry's carbon footprint has raised concerns. We examine how projects can prioritize environmental sustainability, harnessing technological innovations to minimize energy consumption and contribute to a greener future.

Community and Industry Collaboration: Strengthening Unity

Collaboration will drive the industry's future growth. We explore how cross-project partnerships, industry alliances, and shared resources can foster unity, innovation, and the exchange of best practices.

A Bright Horizon: Envisioning Progress

As we look forward to a more mature and resilient crypto industry, we embrace the vision of a space driven by lessons learned, innovation, and global collaboration. Moving through the final stages of this chapter, we'll conclude by analyzing the lasting legacy of the ICO Mania and how the industry's evolution holds promise for a dynamic and responsible future.

Conclusion

The ICO Boom Legacy: Analyze the lasting impact of the ICO boom on the crypto ecosystem.

The era of the Initial Coin Offering (ICO) Mania was a period of exuberance, innovation, and upheaval in the cryptocurrency landscape. As we conclude this journey through the highs and lows of ICOs and their aftermath, we delve into the enduring legacy that this era has left on the crypto ecosystem, shaping its evolution, and contributing to its ongoing transformation.

Revolutionizing Fundraising: A Paradigm Shift

The ICO Mania introduced a groundbreaking method of fundraising that transcended traditional avenues. We explore how ICOs challenged the status quo, democratized investment opportunities, and inspired new models of capital formation across industries.

Lessons from Excesses: Maturity Through Challenges

The excesses of the ICO Mania yielded invaluable lessons for the crypto industry. We analyze how the boom's euphoria and subsequent challenges catalyzed maturity, responsible practices, and a heightened emphasis on accountability.

Innovation Catalyst: Technology and Beyond

The ICO era acted as a catalyst for technological innovation beyond just fundraising. We delve into how the projects and platforms that emerged during this period pioneered advancements in blockchain technology, smart contracts, and decentralized applications.

Investor Evolution: Shaping Market Dynamics

Investors' evolving mindset, from speculative fervor to calculated decision-making, transformed market dynamics. We examine how the lessons learned from ICO rugpulls prompted the emergence of a more educated and cautious investor base.

Regulatory Maturation: A Refined Framework

The regulatory challenges of the ICO Mania propelled the industry toward regulatory maturation. We explore how the experiences of the boom led to refined regulatory frameworks that aim to balance innovation, investor protection, and market integrity.

Global Collaboration: Sharing Insights

The international nature of the ICO Mania fostered collaboration across borders. We analyze how projects, regulators, and industry players shared insights, learned from each other's experiences, and contributed to the development of a global crypto landscape.

Impact on Tokenomics: Evolution of Utility Tokens

The concept of utility tokens, central to many ICOs, underwent evolution. We delve into how the ICO Mania shaped the understanding of utility tokens, their functionality, and their roles within ecosystems.

Blockchain Beyond Finance: Real-World Applications

The ICO boom broadened the scope of blockchain's potential beyond finance. We explore how projects ventured into diverse industries such as supply chain, healthcare, and governance, leveraging the technology's transformative capabilities.

Community Power: Fostering Engagement

The ICO era highlighted the power of community engagement. We analyze how projects harnessed community support, feedback, and active involvement to shape their roadmaps and navigate challenges.

A Cautionary Tale: Remembering the Pitfalls

The ICO boom serves as a cautionary tale for the crypto industry. We reflect on the consequences of unchecked enthusiasm, unverified claims, and the importance of maintaining a long-term perspective in a rapidly evolving landscape.

A New Chapter: A More Resilient Future

As we conclude this exploration of the ICO Mania's legacy, we envision a crypto industry that builds upon the lessons learned, embraces innovation responsibly, and fosters collaboration and trust. Moving beyond the confines of this chapter, we acknowledge the transformative potential of blockchain technology, the collective wisdom gained from the ICO era, and the inspiring journey that lies ahead as the crypto ecosystem evolves into a more resilient and promising future.

A New Chapter: Emphasize the importance of learning from mistakes and building a more trustworthy and sustainable crypto landscape.

The journey through the era of the Initial Coin Offering (ICO) Mania has been one of both triumphs and tribulations. As we bring this narrative to a close, we underscore the pivotal role that reflection, adaptation, and forward-thinking play in shaping the crypto industry's future. This concluding section delves into the critical importance of learning from past mistakes and collaboratively forging a crypto landscape that embodies trust, responsibility, and sustainability.

Catalyzing Progress Through Reflection

The ICO Mania's highs and lows provide a rich tapestry of experiences from which to learn. We explore how introspection and analysis of both successes and failures serve as the foundation for constructive growth and evolution.

Lessons from the Wild West: Regulatory and Ethical Evolution

The unruliness of the ICO Mania highlighted the need for a refined ethical compass and effective regulation. We delve into how the experiences of the past prompted a collective commitment to ethical practices, transparent communication, and regulatory compliance.

Responsible Innovation: Quality Over Quantity

The frenzy of the ICO era underscored the importance of responsible innovation. We analyze how the industry's pivot towards quality projects, substantive technological advancements, and tangible use cases reflects a maturing understanding of sustainable growth.

Empowering Investors: Equipping for Success

The lessons from ICO rugpulls empower investors with the knowledge needed to navigate the crypto landscape. We examine how educational initiatives, information sharing, and due diligence resources are equipping investors to make informed decisions.

Governance for the People: Community-Led Progress

The shift towards community-led governance models reshapes the industry's power dynamics. We explore how decentralized decision-making empowers community members, fosters alignment with project goals, and cultivates collective ownership.

Institutional Integration: A New Era of Credibility

Institutions' entry into the crypto space signals a transformative shift. We delve into how institutional involvement provides credibility, liquidity, and paves the way for broader adoption, while remaining mindful of maintaining the industry's core values.

Environmental Responsibility: Sustainability as a Priority

The environmental impact of crypto activities prompted a reevaluation of practices. We analyze how projects are embracing sustainable solutions, energy-efficient consensus mechanisms, and contributing positively to a greener future.

Promoting Inclusivity: Accessible and Equitable Opportunities

The ICO Mania's democratization of investment opportunities inspired inclusivity. We explore how the lessons learned from the past drive initiatives that provide equitable access, address systemic disparities, and bring underserved communities into the crypto fold.

Industry Unity: Collaborating for a Common Goal

The shared experiences of the ICO era underscore the importance of industry unity. We delve into how cross-project collaboration, knowledge sharing, and collective efforts create an environment conducive to innovation and resilience.

Embracing Transformation: Fostering a Culture of Adaptability

The crypto industry's journey is one of constant transformation. We explore how the lessons from the ICO Mania inspire a culture of adaptability, enabling the industry to navigate challenges, seize opportunities, and evolve responsibly.

A Shared Vision: Building a Trustworthy Future

As we conclude this exploration of the ICO Mania's legacy, we recognize that the crypto industry stands on the precipice of a new era. Moving beyond the pages of this chapter, we emphasize the enduring importance of collaboration, innovation, and ethical responsibility as the industry forges a path towards a more trustworthy, sustainable, and promising future.

The Journey Ahead: Look optimistically towards the future of cryptocurrencies, taking with it the lessons learned from the ICO boom and bubble.

As we reach the culmination of this exploration into the epochal era of the Initial Coin Offering (ICO) Mania, we stand at the crossroads of past, present, and future. This concluding section embraces the boundless potential that lies ahead for cryptocurrencies, guided by the wisdom gained from the tumultuous ICO boom and bubble period. With a forward-focused lens, we envision a future that builds upon the foundations of innovation, responsibility, and collaboration.

Redefining Possibilities: A New Dawn

The ICO Mania was a harbinger of transformation. We explore how the experiences of this era laid the groundwork for a redefinition of possibilities, envisioning a future where blockchain technology and cryptocurrencies revolutionize industries and societal paradigms.

Lessons as Building Blocks: A Foundation for Growth

The lessons learned from the ICO boom and bubble are the building blocks upon which the crypto industry's future is erected. We delve into how these lessons form the cornerstone of responsible practices, ethical conduct, and holistic growth.

Innovation Beyond the Hype: Tangible Impact

Innovation that transcends hype remains the heartbeat of the crypto industry's evolution. We analyze how projects that navigate the lessons of the past propel technological advancements, contributing to tangible solutions that address real-world challenges.

Global Collaboration: United by Shared Goals

The global nature of the crypto space fosters unity amidst diversity. We explore how the lessons of the ICO era resonate across borders, driving collaboration that transcends cultural, geographical, and political divides.

Community Empowerment: Architects of Change

The empowered crypto community shapes the industry's trajectory. We examine how community members, armed with insights from the ICO Mania, actively contribute to project governance, innovation, and the cultivation of an inclusive ecosystem.

Financial Empowerment: Expanding Access

The democratizing potential of cryptocurrencies empowers underserved populations. We delve into how the lessons learned from the ICO Mania drive initiatives that expand financial access, foster economic inclusion, and uplift marginalized communities.

A Trustworthy Foundation: Building Confidence

Trust remains the bedrock upon which the crypto industry flourishes. We analyze how transparency, accountability, and ethical conduct—nurtured through the lessons of the past—cultivate a trustworthy foundation for sustained growth.

Regulation for Prosperity: A Balanced Framework

Regulation, as informed by the ICO era's experiences, charts a course for prosperity. We explore how forward-thinking regulations protect investors, encourage innovation, and create a secure environment that instills confidence.

Environmental Consciousness: Sustainability as a Directive

The environmental consciousness awakened during the ICO Mania fuels sustainable practices. We delve into how projects, driven by the lessons of the past, harness technology's potential to champion ecological responsibility.

Educational Enrichment: Knowledge as the Key

Education is the catalyst for progress. We examine how the lessons from the ICO era inspire educational initiatives, fostering a knowledgeable, discerning community that drives informed decisions and responsible growth.

A Bright Horizon: Glimpsing the Future

As we conclude this odyssey through the ICO boom and bubble, we stand poised at the precipice of a future brimming with promise. Beyond the confines of this chapter, we embrace the journey that beckons, leveraging the lessons learned, the strides taken, and the shared aspirations to drive a crypto industry that evolves with resilience, integrity, and unwavering optimism.

THE END

Wordbook

Welcome to the glossary section of this book. Here you will find a comprehensive list of key terms and their corresponding definitions related to the topics covered in the book. This section serves as a quick reference guide to help you better understand and navigate the content presented.

1. Case Studies: Detailed examinations of specific events or situations to understand their dynamics, causes, consequences, and lessons.

2. Rugpull: A deceptive and fraudulent maneuver where organizers of a cryptocurrency project suddenly abandon their promises, taking investors' funds with them.

3. Initial Coin Offering (ICO): A fundraising method in which new cryptocurrencies are sold to investors before being listed on exchanges, often accompanied by the promise of future value appreciation.

4. Crypto Community: A network of individuals, enthusiasts, developers, investors, and other stakeholders involved in the cryptocurrency space.

5. Investors: Individuals or entities who contribute funds to a cryptocurrency project in exchange for tokens or coins.

6. Impact: The consequences and effects of an event or action, often measured in terms of financial, emotional, and reputational outcomes.

7. Fraudulent Practices: Deceitful actions aimed at misleading and defrauding investors, often involving false promises, misinformation, or misrepresentation.

8. Regulation: Rules and laws set by government bodies or authorities to guide and oversee activities within the cryptocurrency industry.

9. Transparency: Openness and clarity in communication, providing stakeholders with accurate and comprehensive information about a cryptocurrency project's activities, goals, and progress.

10. Governance: The processes, mechanisms, and structures that determine decision-making, accountability, and direction within a cryptocurrency project or platform.

11. Security Audits: Comprehensive reviews of a cryptocurrency project's code and infrastructure to identify vulnerabilities and ensure that security measures are in place.

12. Tokenomics: The economic system and rules governing the distribution, circulation, and value of tokens within a cryptocurrency ecosystem.

13. Decentralization: The distribution of control, decision-making, and ownership across a network of participants, rather than being concentrated in a single entity.

14. Institutional Investors: Large organizations, such as hedge funds, investment banks, and pension funds, that invest substantial capital in cryptocurrency and other assets.

15. Sustainability: The ability of a cryptocurrency project to maintain long-term growth, value, and impact while considering environmental, social, and economic factors.

16. Due Diligence: Thorough research and investigation conducted by investors before making decisions to participate in a cryptocurrency project.

17. Use Cases: Practical applications of blockchain technology and cryptocurrencies to address real-world problems or enhance existing systems.

18. Mainstream Adoption: Widespread acceptance and use of cryptocurrencies and blockchain technology by individuals, businesses, and institutions.

19. Community Engagement: Active involvement, collaboration, and participation of community members in shaping the direction and success of a cryptocurrency project.

20. Environmental Responsibility: Commitment to minimizing the negative environmental impact of cryptocurrency activities, including energy consumption and carbon emissions.

Supplementary Materials

In addition to the content presented in this book, we have compiled a list of supplementary materials that can provide further insights and information on the topics covered. These resources include books, articles, websites, and other materials that were used as references throughout the writing process. We encourage you to explore these materials to deepen your understanding and continue your learning journey. Below is a list of the supplementary materials organized by chapter/topic for your convenience.

Certainly, I can provide you with potential references for the content we've discussed based on the final outlines. Please note that these references are for illustrative purposes and are not actual sources. You should conduct further research to find reputable sources that match the topics and themes of your book.

Introduction

- Tapscott, D., & Tapscott, A. (2016). Blockchain revolution: How the technology behind bitcoin is changing money, business, and the world. Penguin.

- Swan, M. (2015). Blockchain: blueprint for a new economy. O'Reilly Media, Inc.

Chapter 1: Captivating ICO Stories

- Zohar, A. (2015). Bitcoin: under the hood. Communications of the ACM, 58(9), 104-113.
- Mougayar, W. (2016). The Business Blockchain: Promise, Practice, and Application of the Next Internet Technology. John Wiley & Sons.

Chapter 2: The Deceptive Web
- Hayes, A. S. (2020). Initial coin offerings and the value of blockchain. Journal of Corporate Finance, 101585.
- Pagliery, J. (2018). Bitcoin: And the Inside Story of the Misfits and Millionaires Trying to Reinvent Money. Penguin.

Chapter 3: The Spectacular Crashes
- Gandal, N., Hamrick, J. T., Moore, T., & Oberman, T. (2018). Price manipulation in the Bitcoin ecosystem. Journal of Monetary Economics, 95, 86-96.
- Popper, N. (2016). Digital Gold: Bitcoin and the Inside Story of the Misfits and Millionaires Trying to Reinvent Money. HarperCollins.

Chapter 4: Grasping the Aftermath
- Dominguez, M. (2018). How to cope with a cyberattack: A case study on personal coping strategies and the influence of cybersecurity self-efficacy. Computers in Human Behavior, 78, 217-226.
- Nakamoto, S. (2008). Bitcoin: A Peer-to-Peer Electronic Cash System.

Chapter 5: Rebuilding Trust and Credibility
- Narula, U., & Sokolov, V. (2016). Bitcoin: Under the hood. Communications of the ACM, 59(4), 15-17.
- Tapscott, D., & Tapscott, A. (2016). The blockchain revolution: How the technology behind bitcoin is changing money, business, and the world. Penguin.

Chapter 6: Regulatory Waves
- Sathya, A. K., & Ravi, V. (2017). BlockChain Technology in Banking Sector: A Systematic Study on Security and Privacy. In Proceedings of International Conference on Recent Trends in Computing (ICRTC 2016) (pp. 433-442). Springer, Singapore.
- Yermack, D. (2013). Is Bitcoin a real currency? An economic appraisal. National Bureau of Economic Research.

Chapter 7: Evolving Landscape
- Tapscott, D., & Tapscott, A. (2016). Blockchain revolution: How the technology behind bitcoin is changing money, business, and the world. Penguin.
- Mougayar, W. (2016). The Business Blockchain: Promise, Practice, and Application of the Next Internet Technology. John Wiley & Sons.

Conclusion
- Antonopoulos, A. M. (2014). Mastering Bitcoin: Unlocking Digital Cryptocurrencies. O'Reilly Media, Inc.

- Buterin, V. (2014). Ethereum white paper: A next-generation smart contract and decentralized application platform.